The Girl I Buried

The Woman I Birthed.

Sukriti Taneja

BookLeaf Publishing

India | USA | UK

Made with ❤ on the BookLeaf Publishing Platform
www.bookleafpub.in
www.bookleafpub.com

Dedication

To my family,
for the love, the ache, the laughter, the belief and the lessons.

And to life,
thank you for the curveballs.
They made the writing better.

Preface

This one's for her.
The 13-year-old who scribbled poems in class margins,
reread every line like it might one day matter,
and believed, quietly, stubbornly,
that her words would live in a book someday.

It took heartbreaks, healing, curveballs and coffee-
stained drafts,
but she made it. I made it.

These poems carry every version of me:
the girl with the paper wings,
the teenager who came undone,
the woman still figuring it out.

This isn't just poetry. It's proof.
That softness survives.
That stories save.
That the dream was worth it.

And if you're holding this, maybe it's time you believed
in yours too.
Split into three parts: childhood, adolescence, and
womanhood,

this book is a love letter to growing up, and to the girl who did it out loud.

Acknowledgements

To the people who held me when I didn't know how to hold myself, thank you.

Thank you for the laughter, the silences, the scoldings, the late-night "you've got this" calls, and the mornings you didn't let me quit. I'm here because you stayed.

And to you, reader, stranger, kindred spirit. If you see yourself in even one line, this was always for you too.

Paper Wings

Fancy crayons coloured cheap white sheets,
A mediocre house full of giggles and dreams.
No inheritance, no trunk full of gold,
Just two hearts, full of love, brave and bold.

No fancy dinners, no beachside breaks,
But the freedom to colour outside every line I'd make.
Our walls wore my art with quiet pride,
No scoldings, just sheer delight.

The power would go, the night would creep,
So we'd drag out quilts and laugh ourselves to sleep.
The balcony turned into a starlit bed,
With stories and silence gently overhead.

Our luxuries weren't bought, they were made.
Time, attention, and love that stayed.
Truly a childhood that saw secondhand grace,
Yet so full of first-hand love in every space.

Even with nothing, they built me whole,
With fire in my spirit and art in my soul.

The world outside was vast and wild,

But they raised a free, untamed child.
And so, with their love, they sewed me paper wings,
Strong enough to stride, yet rooted in where I begin.

The Clubhouse

On the terrace, we built our own little world,
A tent, a pinboard, our rainbow-coloured abode.
A folder of sheets to colour all day,
With pencils and puzzles, scattered in play.

Evenings were magic, just her and me,
Till clouds rolled in, wild as the sea.
We'd rush to save our world so small,
And Mum and Dad would come, carrying it all.

It wasn't grand, nor did it glitter in gold,
But in every humble moment, our love shone bold.
And though the tent's long packed and our childhood's gone,
The safety of those days forever lingers on.

My First Best Friend

I was five, with a tricycle and too much love to give,
drawn to the dogs that made our lane come alive.
Each evening, I'd ride, their leashes looped tight,
two furry copilots, my heart taking flight.

"Can we get a dog too?" I asked with a grin.
Dad said, "They're a task. Where do we begin?"
But hearts are strange things, they bend and they break,
and sometimes they soften for a little girl's sake.

He watched from the window, arms folded, still,
Something inside him shifting against his will.
And then came Tyson, with eyes full of grace,
A pointy-eared boy with a soldier's face.

He didn't bark much, didn't need to at all,
He'd show up like magic whenever I'd call.
He let me dress him, cry into his fur,
and lay by my feet when life was a blur.

I didn't know love could have four legs and a tail,
but there he was, my first best friend.

The Sky I Spoke To

I used to talk to the sky like a friend,
Asked it if clouds ever get tired of pretend.
If the stars ever blink when no one can see,
If the moon keeps notes of girls like me.

I'd lie on the grass and whisper my dreams,
Told the wind my plans and faraway schemes.
Sometimes, I'd ask how birds just *know*
When to leave, when to stay or where to go?

I'd wonder if flowers feel fear when they bloom,
Or if the rain ever cries alone in its room.
I'd ask why grown-ups forget how to play,
Why time runs fast and night eats the day.

No answers came, just the silence and sky,
But it felt like someone heard me try.
And maybe that's all wonder ever is,
A whisper sent out, just to exist.

The Year Magic Got Quiet

I once believed in Christmas with my whole chest,
Taped my list to the fridge and hoped for the best.
Trusted Mum would call the big man that night,
While I put a sock on the balcony just right.

A tenner from the tooth fairy would find my bed,
While I dreamed of stars and stories she said.
The sound of the watchman's stick made me dash to
Dad.
Every knock, every creak was a code to be cracked.

But magic fades quietly around twelve or so,
When truth knocks softly, asking what you know.
Santa was Mum. The fairy, dad.
The watchman was doing his job, tired alas.

I miss how easily I'd fall for delight,
How hope felt simple, and I knew wrong from right.
Now I light my own lamps to keep out the fright,
But oh, how I long for that old kind of night.

Always in Front

I was always in front, assembly line one,
where the sun hit first and the speeches begun.
First in class photos, first on the seating chart,
A little girl playing the smallest part.

I hated the stares, the nickname parade,
the measuring game we played every day.
But looking back now, it wasn't so bad;
to be the first face at every affair.

Always grounded, always apart,
A small frame with a different heart.
I stood out in lines, and that made me see,
How different can hold its own quiet dignity.

The Mirror Changed First

At thirteen, my curls grew louder than I could bear.
Straight hair became silence, the kind I longed to wear.
It started asking questions I wasn't ready to meet.
It started asking questions I couldn't believe.
Was this how childhood ends?
No loud bang, but a stare I can't meet again.

Black sheep

One cigarette.
One mistake.
And just like that,
I was the only one who paid.

My mother,
a teacher, found out first.
Ashamed and disappointed,
my parents said nothing at all.
Their silence much longer than the punishment.

My "friends" turned their heads,
then their backs.
Like I was a mistake
they could afford to forget.

So I picked up a pen.
Not to be heard,
but to survive.

And that's how writing
became the first thing
that didn't leave my sight.

X, Y, and Why

Maths made me feel
like my brain was in the wrong body.
Like the numbers were all whispering
secrets I wasn't cool enough to know.

I'd stare at the board
like it had personally betrayed me.
X and Y,
always looking for things
they should've kept track of themselves.

I hated maths.
Not because I didn't try.
But because no one cared
why I couldn't understand.

They marked my worth
in red pens and percentage signs.
And all I wanted
was to be good at something
you couldn't solve with a formula.

Delirious Troublemaker

I was the girl
with the "not appropriate for school" socks,
the skirt rolled too high,
the hair no one could tame.

I carried a camera, not a calculator.
Didn't care much
for academia or applause.

PTMs felt like courtrooms,
every adult laying blame,
"She won't pass," they'd whisper,
"What future will she claim?"

But rebellion was my friend,
doubt became my fuel.
Each sideways glance pushed me
to break every spoken rule.

And so, somehow,
this troublemaker took flight,
landing softly on the toppers' lists
with a college they'd die to write.

Turns out, trouble looks good in hindsight.

12

Hidden Scars

There was a year
my sleeves spoke more than I did.

I smiled.
I showed up.

But pieces of me
kept slipping away.

And so for the stories
I cannot say out loud,
I'll paint them into poetry,
and art so proud.

Letting Go

I detach sometimes,
slowly at first,
and then all at once.

I think,
and think,
and think,
until my thoughts know no bounds.

Still,
why do these fragmented moments
keep me awake?
Gripping onto me
like a sudden brake.

I tell myself it's too fast, too soon,
but then, the gentle smile on your face
undoes my swoon.

And yet,
this brace face I wear
seems to shut even you out,
unaware of everything that haunts me now.

You say you know me best.
But do you notice the shift in my steps?
The silence in my ways?

And so, I detach,
slowly at first,
and then all at once.

An Abode for Tyson

And just like that,
I too will disappear one day.
My ashes will scatter
as the wind rushes to do.

No last words,
no proper goodbyes,
I too will disappear into the night sky.

I only hope your heart can still feel my love
when I can no longer provide.

I only hope to meet you again on the other side.

The Tragedy of First

He loved someone else.
I loved the idea of being chosen.

I made excuses
and called it patience.

It wasn't love.
It was hoping,
loud and lonely.

But I stayed.
Because first love
doesn't know
when to leave.

Lockdown

Yet another day begins
with the struggle to crawl out of bed
at quarter past twelve.
Tea in hand, I scroll through Instagram.

The days are free,
yet somehow always full.
It's been four long months of captivity.

"Oh, what a life it would be
if every day were a weekend,"
I once sighed.
Little did I know, wishes could rot.

As the hours blur, my mind drifts,
to the darkest corners that exist.
The mistrust,
the past,
the slamming,
leave me crying on my knees.

It's strange how quickly time changes,
how easily bonds break.

Lullabies that once put me to sleep
are now replaced with cigarettes
and whiskey neat.

Each day is a struggle, each moment, a war.
And yet, with every sunrise,
I pick up my armour again,
and sip on my hot morning tea.

Knocking

So much to be,
so little time.
I have much to prove;
not to the world,
but the people I call mine.

To be strong,
but never cold.
To show up,
even when I fold.

To carry dreams
I didn't invent,
and turn them into
time well spent.

And still, make space for softness,
joy, and me.

So much to be.
And yet, still learning
how to just be.

Four Suitcases

I packed my life into four suitcases
and told myself this was growth.
That airports were just places,
not beginnings of guilt yet to unfold.

Independence wasn't glorious.
It was dishes at 1 a.m.,
cold pasta,
missed birthdays,
and unread messages
I didn't have the energy to open.

I kept the guilt folded neatly,
between job shifts and late-night essays,
told myself
this is what daughters do,
trade comfort for opportunity.

And when I came back,
the doormat felt too clean.
The house too familiar.
The hugs too short.

Coming home was harder.

Being home, even more.
I wasn't who I was,
but you still saw her.

So I smiled again,
and quietly unpacked
the woman I'd become,
and was still learning to hone.

A love letter to Jerry

He came five years after the ache,
when love felt too fragile to risk again.
No one said it aloud,
but something didn't quite feel okay.

And then you came,
big ears, tiny paws,
walking in like you owned us all.

Your love is not shy.
And neither are you.
Full of drama,
full of sass;
you know it's true.

A heart of gold.
A love so pure.
You fixed something
You made us whole.

You are the heart of this house,
the glue that holds us,
the joy in our slowest hours,
and the mischief that makes us roar.

You are perfection.
You are comfort.
You are chaos.
You are hope.

You're everything to me,
and so much more.

Love Too Loud

I often joke
that I'll never find someone
who loves me
like my dad loves my mom.

He worships her.
In the quiet ways;
that just scream out loud.

Love, in our house,
was never shy,
it echoed, just right.

It lingered
in matching cups of coffee,
long drives and shopping sprees.

It was glances across rooms
when no one else was looking.
Dancing without music,
arguing without malice,
forgiving without keeping score.

And now,

every time someone offers me less,
I know exactly why it won't work.

Because I saw what love could be
before I ever felt it.

And the bar?
Well, it was set *toohigh* at home.

Coming Undone

I am a girl,
Raised by parents who fought against all odds,
To give their daughters a life they never had,
A life filled with dreams they could only wish for.

I am a girl,
With dreams bigger than my years,
Fueled by a hunger for success waiting to appear.

I am a girl,
With a heart broken more times than I can count,
Yet still open, still willing to feel.

I am a girl,
Who cries at the end of every rom-com,
Worships *Jaane Tu Ya Jaane Na*, craving a love that
consumes and calms.

I am a girl,
Who met someone who makes me feel blessed,
To know a love that touches the soul and rests.

I am a girl,
Who dreams of marriage, family, kids,

And a house filled with dogs' joyous mess.

I am a girl,
With a taste for adventure, a rush that won't quit,
And a curiosity that pushes me past every shadow, every hit.

I am the girl,
Who laughs the loudest in the room,
Yet wonders if her smile truly blooms.

I am the girl,
Who would jump from a 30-foot cliff,
Just to feel the thrill that makes me feel real.

I am a girl,
Learning to navigate a world cloaked in shadows.

I am a girl,
Growing into a woman, unsure if it's okay to want it all,
Knowing life isn't a paradise, I learned that young.

So, why wait for destiny
When I can create the life I want?

In the end, the choice is mine, and mine alone;
To hold on to betrayals or to see the good in it all.

Privilege is tricky; I've known this for long.
It's more than money, power, or the status quo,
It's the freedom to dream, a privilege I was handed down.

I am a pampered daughter,
A sister, loved unconditionally, kept safe from harm.
Not a girl's girl, but a girl with boys who feel like home.

For all the norms I fight against,
The toughest ones live in my mind.

I am more than a girl;
I am a woman who wants it all.

And so, I manifest my truth, my call.

It's okay to dream,
It's okay to strive,
It's okay to chase every spark that makes me feel alive.

It's okay to say, "No, thank you. This isn't for me."
It's okay to be selfish, it's okay to be free.

It's okay to be more than the girl who believed in fairy tales.

It's okay to be both fierce and tender, unafraid to fail.

It's okay to let someone care for me,
Not because I need them, but because I deserve the love I
seek.

It's okay to silence the voices that say I can't have it all,
Because we were made to rise, to live, to thrive, and have
it all.

To be a Woman

The world is not roses and petals,
this, I've come to know.

To be a woman
is to be soft,
and yet, so bold.

It is to know your voice matters.
It is to be called
"too much" and "not enough",
sometimes all at once.

It is to carry generations in your spine,
and patience in your palms.

It is to come undone,
to rebuild,
to rise,
again,
and again,
and again.

www.ingramcontent.com/pod-product-compliance
Lightning Source LLC
LaVergne TN
LVHW051242200726

843510LV00011B/1652